ALL ABOUT

Mariano Rivera

Jorge Iber & Raquel Iber

D1173284

BLUE
RIVER
PRESS

Indianapolis, Indiana

All About Mariano Rivera
Copyright © Jorge Iber, Raquel Iber, 2020

Published by Blue River Press
Indianapolis, Indiana
www.brpressbooks.com

Distributed by Cardinal Publishers Group
A Tom Doherty Company, Inc.
www.cardinalpub.com

ISBN: 978-1-68157-124-9

Cover Design: David Miles
Book Design: Rick Korab
Cover Artist: Nicole McCormick Santiago
Editor: Dani McCormick
Illustrator: Colleen Deignan

Printed in the United States of America

10 9 8 7 6 5 4 3 2 1   20 21 22 23 24 25 26 27 28

CONTENTS

ALL ABOUT

Mariano Rivera

Born in a poor Panamanian fishing village, Mariano River Jr. did not think he would grow up to be a famous New York Yankees pitcher. In fact, he thought that he would follow his father into the fishing industry. After he replaced a poorly-performing pitcher during an amateur baseball game, the Yankees scout saw his talent.

Mariano Rivera would go on to become a thirteen-time All-Star and five-time World Series

The "core four" who helped lead a great era in Yankees' history. Mariano, Jorge Posada, Andy Pettitte, and Derek Jeter.

champion. He holds two MLB records and has won many other awards. H is a favorite for induction into the Hall of Fame.

Derek Jeter called Mariano "the most mentally tough" teammate he'd ever played with. Rivera easily rose to being a team leader and helping the team recover from losses with dignity, and celebrate wins with humility. When once asked to describe his job, Mariano simply stated, "I get the ball, I throw the ball, and then I take a shower."

After retiring, Mariano devoted himself to philanthropy and his churches. He and his wife Clara sponsor college scholarships, a foundation to provide underprivileged children with educations, and various other projects. He was unanimously voted into the national Baseball Hall of Fame in 2019. The same year, President Trump honored him with the Presidential Medal of Freedom, the highest non-military award in the United States.

CHAPTER ONE

Panamanian Boyhood

Mariano Rivera never thought he would become a baseball player, let alone one of the greatest ever! After he dropped out of high school at the age of 16, he hoped to become a boat mechanic. He worked with his father to save money to go to mechanic school.

Mariano's elementary school was named Centro Basico Victoriano Chacon.

| 1 |

While still in elementary school, Mariano focused on playing soccer and dealing with students who made fun of him because he smelled like fish. Why did Mariano smell of fish? Simple. His father was a fisherman, who caught sardines and then sold them to a plant that made fish meal.

At school students would make fun of Mariano, calling him "fishy boy," and saying that, "I thought we were in school, not on a fishing boat." Such words hurt him, and Mariano often got into fights. "I could've, should've, ignored them. I did not."

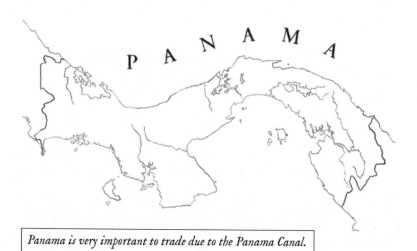

Panama is very important to trade due to the Panama Canal.

The fights, and problems with some teachers, led him to make a poor choice: he left school in the 9th grade.

Mariano did not think about the problems this could cause. He did not get much help from his parents because they too had left school at an early age. He still hoped to not have to work long hours on the boats; that was why he wanted to be a mechanic.

Mariano was born in 1969 in a Panamanian fishing village called Puerto Caimito. Life there was good because he had many family members nearby. Most of the town, he thought, was made up of his aunts, uncles, and cousins.

"It makes for . . . instant . . . playmates when you want to start up a game."

Many families did not have electricity, running water or indoor bathrooms. By the time of Mariano's birth, his family had electricity and running water, but still used an outhouse.

Their house was located near the fish meal plant, making it more difficult to get rid of the "fishy smell." Mariano spent a lot of time by the seashore. At low tide, he, his cousins and friends played soccer and baseball.

Mariano liked soccer more than baseball, but when he got hit in the eye by a soccer ball and lost his vision for a while, he left that sport behind.

Another favorite was a made-up game where the kids put up a piece of cardboard with three holes.

For a time, Mariano actually preferred soccer to baseball.

Then, from far away, they threw rocks through the holes.

"My aim was good," Mariano recalled.

When the tide came in, the boys turned to another "sport;" hunting iguanas with rocks. Again, Mariano had great aim. Many times, the big lizards became part of Rivera's dinner.

Little did the young Mariano Rivera know how his good aim, and practice at throwing rocks to a spot from far away, would change his life and make him a hero to many people around the world.

He would go from not knowing much about baseball history to making a lot of history on his own. He would then use his fame to help many people better their lives.

Iguanas are large lizards with crests. They are found in many places in Central America.

CHAPTER TWO

From a Fishing Boat to the Mound

Panama is an isthmus; a thin strip of land with water on two sides that joins two larger areas of land. The country is in Central America.

Each year about 14,000 ships pass through the Panama Canal.

It is the home of the Panama Canal, built between 1903 and 1914 to join the Caribbean Sea and Pacific Ocean. The United States ran the Canal for many years, then returned it to Panama in 1999.

Working on the canal is a key job in this country, but so are fishing and farming. Mariano Rivera's father did these last two jobs early in his life.

Puerto Caimito is about 25 miles from the Canal and fishing is the main job. The older Mariano Rivera was not born there but came to work as a fisherman when he was 17.

Puerto Caimito is located about twenty-five miles from the canal.

He was born in the town of Darien, near the border with Colombia. He was one of 15 children and worked on his parent's small farm. He would work 11 hours per day, 6 days a week to help his family.

He left school in the sixth grade. Some of Mariano's brothers had moved to Puerto Caimito because fishing paid more than farming. He joined them and took whatever jobs he could to learn to fish.

Soon he met Delia Giron, who was 15 at the time. Mariano saw her washing clothes and heard her singing. They fell in love and got married.

In 1967, the family welcomed a daughter name Delia, then two years later they had Mariano. For the first 17 years of his life, the family lived in a cement house on a dirt road near the shores of the Gulf of Panama.

Mariano remembers that he did not have very much when he was a boy. He played baseball on the shore, and even travelled with a team starting at age 13, but did not get his first glove until he was 16. He got a used glove just before the family left their house by the shore and moved about one-third of a mile away.

Mariano was a good ball player, but at that time no one was saying that he could be a pro like Rod Carew, Rennie Stennett, or Manny Sanguillen—baseball legends from Panama.

Mariano's favorite time of the year was Christmas; though he did not get many toys. For years he got the same gift: a cap gun. He liked to fire it while he watched his favorite TV show: The Lone Ranger.

While the Lone Ranger was the star, Mariano liked the Ranger's helper, Tonto, because he was "smart and loyal and so humble that he doesn't care about getting credit." Mariano learned much from how Tonto acted.

Mariano's father was a good provider and showed his son how to work hard and stick to a job; even when times were tough. He would get up at 5:00 on Monday mornings and stayed out all week on his boat, the Lisa, working 12-14 hours each day.

At the age of 18, Mariano went to work for his father. He made $50 per week; most of this he would save to go to mechanic school.

There were three events, however, that changed his life in these years. He got good advice from his future wife Clara Diaz Chacon, and there were two fishing accidents aboard the Lisa.

Clara and Mariano had known each other since they were in kindergarten. She was upset after Mariano dropped out of high school and stopped speaking with him.

Mariano was going out to dance clubs in the nearby city of Chorrera. One night they ran into each other and Clara spoke with him about her concerns.

These are the types of fishing boats found in Puerto Caimito.

Clara feared that Mariano would get hurt because there were often fights; some of the boys at the club even had knives!

Mariano recalled that one time someone went after him with a machete. He knew Clara was right and that he had to change his behavior. Mariano also knew that he and Clara were falling in love, and he did not like being away from her when he was out on the Lisa most of the week. Still, he had to work to help his father and his family.

The first accident happened early one morning as the Lisa was taking on tons of sardines. The time was around 4:00 a.m.

Normally, fishermen did not work at this time because it was too dark, but there were too many fish in the water to pass up this chance.

As they brought in the haul, a rope broke and a piece of equipment slammed into Mariano's uncle Miguel. He was badly hurt. For one month, he hung on, but died.

Although the family was very sad, the only way to make money was to fish. A few days after Miguel's funeral, the Lisa was back at sea.

About one year later, another tragedy struck. The Lisa's pumps, which take water out so the boat could stay afloat, broke down and the craft started sinking. At the time, the boat was about 1000 feet from shore.

Just then, the pumps started working and Mariano thought all would be well.

Not quite. Once again, the pumps shut down and then the motor stopped! By the time Mariano and his father headed for the life boat, they had to go through waist-high water.

Lisa's *sinking changed Mariano's life. He knew he didn't want to be a fisherman forever.*

Behind them, father and son saw the Lisa, the family's only way to make a living, disappear! They were not yet safe, however. The little life boat was tossed by large waves in waters that contained sharks!

The older Mariano, who knew the waters in the Gulf of Panama well, got them to the shore of a beach on the island of Pacheca. They were safely on land! Mariano's father got another boat in time, but for now, the family's fishing season was over.

These two scary moments at sea convinced young Mariano he wanted nothing to do with fishing. He still fixed nets, however.

With time away, he had a chance to play more baseball and his skills got him invited to play for the Panama Oeste Vaqueros (Panama West Cowboys) in the top adult league in Panama.

He played outfield, shortstop, and even catcher; wherever he was needed. He batted second in the lineup and was a good hitter and fast runner. He preferred to play the outfield.

He was playing one day as the Cowboys had a playoff game. Mariano and his teammates thought they would win easily, after all their best pitcher was on the mound. That was not how things turned out.

The starter had a rough day and the other side got many hits and runs. The Cowboys' manager came out of the dugout and looked around to see whom to bring in to pitch. He looked Mariano's way as asked him to come to the mound.

"'Why is he looking at me?' I think. 'He can't mean me. I am not even a pitcher.'"

Little did Mariano know that this would be the first of many times that a manager would call him to the mound. This would be the first step on Mariano's road to becoming one of the greatest pitchers ever.

CHAPTER THREE

Do You Really Expect Me to Believe This?

As he walked toward his manager with the Cowboys, Mariano did not know what to expect.

First, he was scared to be called to the mound. He was not a pitcher; the only spots he had thrown to were holes on a cardboard and at iguanas. These "games" had not prepared him to face batters, right?

The only time he had pitched were a few innings for his local team when he was 14 years old. How could he do this in a playoff game? The manager told him that he knew he was not a pitcher, but the team needed his help.

"Throw strikes, and you'll be fine."

Mariano said he would do his best, after all, he had a good arm and could put the ball where he wanted most of the time. However, he knew that he did not throw very hard, only about 80 to 85 miles per hour or so.

He also felt weird standing on the rubber; the small board on the mound from where a pitcher starts his delivery.

To his surprise, he did very well. He came in during the second inning and went the rest of the game. He did not give up a single run.

He did not do anything fancy: just a fastball to the spots pointed out by his catcher. The Cowboys came back to win, and his manager told Mariano how proud he was of his effort. That, Mariano thought, would be the end of his pitching career.

"Next time out, I will be back at short or left or whatever." Baseball was great, but he was busy fixing nets and thinking about when he could afford to sign up for mechanic school.

About two weeks after this game, Mariano spent a great day on the beach with his family and Clara. When the Riveras returned to their house, two friends from the Cowboys where waiting at the front door. They were Emilio Gaes and Claudio Hernandez, his team's center fielder and catcher.

It turns out that they had spoken with a man named Chico Heron who was a scout. Emilio and Claudio told Chico that Mariano had a good arm and might be a prospect.

He agreed to see what Mariano could do. The tryout would take place in Panama City.

At first, Mariano thought his friends were playing a trick on him. He knew he was not a pitcher, so how could a Major League scout be interested? Then, his teammates brought up an even bigger surprise: the tryout was not just for any scout, but one from the

The Panama City-Colon region is home to about fifty percent of all Panamanians.

New York Yankees, the most legendary team in all of baseball!

Chico scouted Mariano before as an infielder but was not sure he was a prospect because of his hitting. Now, Mariano was really convinced his friends were not telling the truth, but Emilio and Claudio said that this was real.

They had reached out to Chico for two reasons: first, they believed that Mariano had talent; second, if the Yankees signed their friend, they would get some money for having brought the prospect to the club's attention.

Estadio Juan Demostenes Arosemena was where Mariano had his tryout.

It took a while to convince Mariano, but he agreed to go visit with Chico the following day at the ballpark in the nation's capital.

The next day, before he could leave for the tryout, Mariano's father asked him to spend the first part of the day fixing fishing nets. He then caught a bus to Chorrera at about 1:00 in the afternoon. Then, another bus to his destination; an old ballpark in the center of the city.

When he arrived, Mariano did not look very impressive to say the least! He was wearing some old green pants, and a beat-up shirt. He had holes in his shoes.

He remembered thinking, "Hey, look, they're giving a tryout to a hobo."

Chico was willing to give Mariano a chance, but he was at the ballpark to look at another pitcher named Luis Parra. Mariano did not think that this was a chance to change his life, but he would do his best.

He went to the mound, threw a total of nine pitches, and put the ball where he wanted it to go. Chico told Mariano he had done well, and that nine pitches was all he needed to see.

Chico said that he had liked what he saw and wanted Mariano to come back. Chico would also talk to his boss, a man named Herb Raybourn, to see what he had to say.

The rest of the week was just like this first day. Mariano fixed nets, took buses to Panama City, and worked out for Chico and soon, for Herb.

Herb was well known in Puerto Caimito and around the rest of Panama. He had signed other players, including one of Mariano's cousins, Manuel Giron, who spent three years in the minor leagues for the Pittsburgh Pirates.

Manuel did not make it to the Majors and returned to Puerto Caimito. Cousin Manuel did not talk much about his time in professional baseball and Mariano did not ask too many questions. Manuel was now back home working in the fishing industry, just like most of the folks in Puerto Caimito.

On the final day of that week, Mariano got a chance to pitch in a game. Herb told him that he would be the starter. Mariano got loose and went to the mound.

Chico Heron was a famous minor league player.

As he did with the Cowboys, he did not try anything fancy: he just threw fastballs. He did, however, put the ball where he wanted it to go almost every time.

He pitched three innings, struck out five, and gave up only one hit. Chico told him that he had done well, but Mariano would have to wait a little bit until the scouts finished looking at other prospects.

After the game, Herb came over and spoke with Mariano. He said that Mariano had a future as a pitcher.

The next day, Mariano returned to Panama City, and spoke with Herb again. Then the two drove back to Puerto Caimito.

Herb had a suitcase with him as he entered the Riveras' house, and Mariano was curious about what was inside. Herb got down to business quickly.

With Mariano Sr., Delia, and Clara by his side, Mariano heard some wonderful, but also scary, news. Herb offered the young player $2,000 plus

Mariano's childhood home was a very special place to him.

Herb Raybourn was one of the scouts who signed Mariano and started his baseball career.

a glove and spikes to sign a contract with the New York Yankees.

The date was February 17, 1990. This would be a day that both the Rivera family and the Yankees would long remember as this skinny "pitcher" would become one of the greatest of all time at his position and would help lead the Yankees to an era of great success.

CHAPTER FOUR

The Minors, Surgery, and Marriage

Mariano had signed with the Yankees and now began the hard work of making his way up the team's "farm system." In baseball, a "farm" is a place where teams "grow" their future players.

The Yankees hoped Mariano would reach the Major Leagues someday, but that would take a few years. Teams sign many prospects, but not all make it to the Majors. A prospect is expected to "move up" the system, facing better players the higher he goes.

A player like Mariano starts at the lowest level, Rookie League. If they do well, the next step is

A-level. Then, AA. The highest level is AAA; the last stop before the Majors.

Mariano would start his career in what to him was a strange place: Tampa, Florida. Also, he must now speak and write a new language: English.

Mariano, his parents, and a cousin at the airport before his flight to Florida.

Things would not be easy, either on the field or in day-to-day life. At first, he thought he might be able to stay in Panama and play baseball there, but that is not how a farm system works.

Mariano faced many challenges as he started his Yankees career. First, he would be away from his family and Clara and everything he knew in Puerto Caimito.

Next, he had to fly to Florida, and he had never been on a plane before!

Finally, he did not know what to expect from life in the United States. How would he speak with others? How would he get along with teammates and coaches who might not be able to understand him?

Mariano was afraid, but "I try not to let on. I have always been good at hiding my feelings."

Shortly after signing, Mariano began the trip to Panama City for his flight to Miami, Florida and then on to Tampa. His sister Delia, Clara, his mother and father all rode along on the trip to the airport in the capital.

Mariano would not be alone, however. The other

prospect that the Yankees signed, Luis Parra, would be with him. Arriving in Miami, they were happy to find some people who spoke Spanish and directed the young men to the gate for their flight to Tampa.

Tampa was a whole new world. Mariano was amazed by the paved roads and how big the buildings looked! The team put the two Panamanians in a nice hotel, where they would live during the season. Mariano and Luis both had trouble understanding what room service was.

When they were not playing, they mostly stayed in the hotel, and would only go out to eat. If their server at the restaurant did not speak Spanish, then they pointed to the picture of the food they wanted in the menu.

"Iguana dishes were strangely absent," Mariano remembered.

The Yankee team Mariano pitched for was in the Gulf Coast League. The other teams in the league were in smaller cities, such as Dunedin, Clearwater, and Bradenton.

The team traveled by bus, and there was not a lot to do while on the road. Mariano was lucky, however, in that he made a friend named Tim Cooper who studied Spanish in school and became his English teacher.

Mariano was a very good pitcher that season. He still did not throw very hard, but he struck out many hitters and had a very low earned run average (ERA). He wondered how and why things were going so well.

On the last day of the season, he got to pitch against the Pirates and did something unusual: he pitched a no-hitter! This made him the pitcher with the lowest ERA in the league. That earned him a $500 bonus.

After the season, he flew back home. In the off-season, he trained with Chico. His good results in Tampa earned him a move up to A ball in Greensboro, North Carolina.

While happy to move up, there were not too many people in this city who spoke Spanish. He was lucky that his teacher, Cooper, was also promoted to the same team. While learning English, Cooper and Mariano talked about what was important in their lives.

Mariano had never flown before becoming a professional baseball player. Throughout his career, though, he flew hundreds of times.

Mariano, remembering what he learned with his family, said that "what's important is how you treat people." Cooper agreed. This belief would play a large part in Mariano's career and life after baseball.

The season in Greensboro went well, though he lost more games than he won. Mariano had an ERA of 2.75. Anything below a 3.00 is very good.

He did have some problems, however. All during 1991, he had a pain in his elbow, but did not think too much about it and used ice on the elbow often to reduce the pain. Still, he had more important things on his mind.

When he returned to Panama, he continued to train with Chico, but also asked Clara to be his wife. They got married on November 9, 1991. The couple moved in with Clara's mother to save money. Mariano hoped that soon they would be able to build a house of their own.

A good first step toward the house was not only saving money but also continuing to move up the system. He soon got word that the Yankees had decided to move him up to a higher-level A team in Ft. Lauderdale for 1992.

He did well with his new team, but then something happened during one game in August. Mariano threw over to first base to keep a runner close and

Mariano and Clara on their wedding day.

he felt a pop in his arm.

He wanted to continue but the pain did not allow him to pitch anymore. He was sent to Miami for tests. Was his career over just like that?

Like Tonto, he was ready to accept whatever came, though he hoped for the best. "I come at life from a mechanic's mind-set. If you've got a problem, you find it and take care of it."

Mariano's baseball card during his time with the Tampa Yankees.

It turned out that he needed an operation, and that was done on August 27, 1992. He was out of action until spring training in 1993.

The Yankees sent him to Tampa, then to Greensboro to get back in shape. It was in this season in North Carolina when he met another player who would be a big part of the Yankees' success: Derek Jeter.

Another wonderful thing happened in 1993 as Mariano and Clara had their first son, Mariano Rivera, Jr. They were very happy.

As a ballplayer, Mariano continued to make progress and for the 1994 season, he moved up again: this time to the AAA team for the Yankees, in Columbus, Ohio. He was now a proud father, a happy husband, and only one step away from the Major Leagues!

CHAPTER FIVE

The Majors, Back to the Minors, and Miracles

Mariano had a great career, but his time in the minors was not rare. Players often move up to a higher level, get hurt, and get sent back down. That happened to Mariano. Players can also be moved up more than one level in a season. The Yankees moved Mariano from AA, back down to A, to AAA all during 1994!

One day, after pitching for Columbus, his manager called him to his office. It was May of 1995. The manager had bad news: Mariano would no longer play for Columbus.

He had good news, too. The New York Yankees had called, and Mariano was going to the Majors! This is the moment all players in the farm system hope for. Mariano was very happy and called his family to tell them the news.

Mariano in his Columbus Clippers uniform.

Jackie Robinson is one of the most recognizable baseball players because of the role he played in reintegrating the Major Leagues.

Mariano flew to New York City, got to Yankee Stadium, walked into the locker room and saw his uniform: number 42.

That number is notable, as it is important to baseball history. That was Jackie Robinson's number. He was the African American who broke baseball's color line in 1947.

In 1997 the Majors retired 42: that meant no player on any team could ever wear it again. If a player wore 42 before 1997, they could keep it. When he retired in 2013 Mariano was the last player in the Majors to wear 42.

The Yankees then left New York and flew out West. They were to play the Angels in Anaheim. The Yankees' starter was hurt, and Mariano got the call.

He did well at first but ran into trouble in the third inning; giving up two runs. In the fourth the Angels scored three times. Mariano left the mound and was behind, 5 – 0 and New York lost, 10 – 0.

Not a good start! Mariano, however, thought like a mechanic: what do I need to fix? He was sure that the next time he would do better.

He won against Oakland, then did not do well the next two times on the mound. His ERA was 10.20. His manager called Mariano in and told him he needed to do more work in AAA.

He went back to the minors on June 11, 1995. Although sad about having to go back down to Columbus, Mariano was sure that if he worked hard, he would be back with the Yankees.

When he got back to Columbus, his arm did not feel right. The team gave him two weeks to rest before he would play again.

On his next time out, his catcher Jorge Posada thought something was strange: Mariano was throwing a lot harder than ever before! He was now hitting around 96 miles per hour, or even one or two miles more than that.

Mariano's Bible is never far from his side.

Jorge asked Mariano, "What did you eat today?"

Mariano did not think it was something that he ate, instead, he thought it was a gift from God. Since he had not been a pitcher who could throw this fast, Mariano thought of this new speed as being a miracle.

This was not the first miracle Mariano believes God had done in his life. He remembered how he was spared when the *Lisa* sank.

He thinks meeting Clara was another blessing, as she helped him get on the right path and avoid trouble. Later, she was sick with chicken pox a few months before Mariano Jr. was born. The doctor was very worried. Clara, Mariano, and friends prayed very much for the baby's health. Two months before his birth, the doctor said the baby would be fine: and he was.

Mariano has been a very religious man since he was around 18, but it was not a quick process. He saw that a cousin, Vidal Ovalle, had had a great change in his life, and asked him about what had happened. Vidal talked to Mariano about the Bible, and how God's Word changed his life.

Mariano listened, but it took a while for him to give his life fully to God. He called his movement toward God his "baby steps."

About five years later, Mariano was back home during the off-season, and was at church. The pastor asked if anyone wanted to give their life to Christ.

Mariano thought about it and felt that he was called. He was ready. He believed that he was being given the chance to become a totally different person.

Mariano's cleats sport his favorite Bible verse which is Philipians 4:13.

He would no longer feel the anger he had when people made fun and called him "fishy boy." He felt that God had totally changed his life. His beliefs became the guide to all parts of his life, including baseball.

"It is the way I want to pitch, and it is the way I want to live. Today is all we have...Put everything we have into living this moment the best way we can live it. Again, it is simple. Simple is best." As Mariano moved through the rest of his career, this attitude was visible for all to see: in good times and in bad.

On July 3, 1995 Mariano was called up to the Yankees one more time. He would never be in the minor leagues again. This time, he was not as excited as when he got the call. He was ready and knew what he needed to do to play in the Majors.

He packed his bags and boarded a flight to Boston, and then to Chicago, where the Yankees were playing the White Sox. In his bag were his clothes, gear, and a red-leather Bible that Clara had given him.

Mariano started the next day against Chicago. He did not feel that he was throwing differently, but the White Sox had trouble hitting him. He went all the way to the eighth-inning, and the Yankees led, 3-0. His manager took him out and brought in the closer, John Wetteland, to finish the game.

Mariano remained with the team for the rest of the year and won five games. His ERA at the end of 1995 was 5.51. That is not great, but much better than when he was up back in May. The Yankees won their division and went to the playoffs against the Seattle Mariners.

Jeter's rookie year was 1995, and he credits Mariano for teaching him how to be a major-leaguer.

The Yankees won the first game of the series in their home stadium. Then in Game Two, Mariano got his chance. He was called to relieve Wetteland in the 12th inning.

The Yankees were losing, 5-4. New York tied the game in the bottom of the inning, and Mariano then pitched the 13th, 14th, and 15th innings. The Yankees scored in the bottom of the 15th and won.

The playoff against Seattle did not go the Yankees' way. They lost, three games to two. Mariano pitched in Game 5 and struck out the hitter he faced. The Mariners won in the 11th inning.

Although on the losing side, Mariano was very happy with how he did. He pitched 5.1 innings and did not allow a run in high pressure games! He was anxious to see what would come next.

"I don't know where the Lord's grace and mercy will take me from here, but I know it will be rich, and know that I am not alone."

There was still one more miracle to come on the mound for Mariano, and it would happen in 1997, but 1996 would also be a great year too!

CHAPTER SIX

The Cutter, Another World Series, and "Enter Sandman"

Pitchers have always tried to make baseballs move in different ways. If a pitcher can make the ball move in a tricky manner, he has a better chance of getting batters out.

For most, this takes a lot of practice. For Mariano Rivera, the pitch that made him a great closer appeared just like his increased speed. He believed it was yet another miracle.

In 1996 the Yankees got a new manager, Joe Torre. This meant that even though Mariano did well in 1995 he would have to prove himself again and in a different way: he would now come out of the bullpen.

Mariano was the "set up" reliever; that meant that he came in just before the closer (Wetteland) who finished the game. He did very well. With his increased speed, it was difficult for hitters to catch up to his fastball. After almost two months of the season, Mariano had an ERA of 0.83. He even went a total of 15 innings without giving up a hit.

Many Yankee fans believed that he should have been in the All-Star Game, but he was not. The fans were mad, but Mariano was glad for the opportunity to return to Panama and spend time with Clara who was having another baby; a boy they named Jafet.

1996 was quite a year for the Yankees. The team won their division and made the playoffs. Mariano had a great year too! He won eight games and finished with 130 strikeouts in 107 innings. Anytime a pitcher gets more than one strikeout per inning, he is doing very well! His ERA was excellent: 2.09.

The Yankees went into the playoffs against the Texas Rangers and won, then beat the Baltimore

Orioles in the finals of the American League. Mariano did his part, pitching a total of 8.2 innings in the two series, with an ERA of 0.00. The Yankees then played the Atlanta Braves in the World Series.

The Braves won the first two games at Yankee Stadium, and New York was in trouble. The Yankees battled back, however, and won the next four. Wetteland closed out all the Yankees' wins. Mariano pitched well, too. He went 5.2 innings and had an ERA of 1.59.

In 1997, Mariano had a new role: he was now the closer, as John Wetteland joined the Texas Rangers. This was a big moment in Mariano's life and career, and he felt great pressure.

At the start of the year, the Yankees lost 10 of their first 15 games, and Mariano failed to close out three of his first six chances. Did the Yankees make a mistake in selecting Mariano as their closer?

Joe Torre called Mariano into his office. He was worried that his young pitcher was trying too hard on the mound.

"You need to be Mariano Rivera. Nothing more, nothing less. You are our closer."

Mariano was grateful for the pep talk and felt much better. His results changed quickly, and he saved his next twelve games. Then, another miracle happened.

In June, the Yankees were in Detroit for a series against the Tigers and Mariano was playing catch with pitcher Ramiro Mendoza. Just as had happened with Jorge Posada, Ramiro noticed something strange about Mariano's pitches.

As they loosened up, Mariano's throws did something strange: they were moving sideways, or cutting across the plate, just at the last moment. The pitch looked like a fastball, but it had a lot of movement.

It took a few tries for Mariano to get control of the pitch, but he soon did. Here was a great weapon for a pitcher! Mariano saw this as another gift from God.

He did not think he was doing anything differently, but the results were amazing. He soon was the most feared closer in baseball. By the end of the year, he had won six games, and saved 43. His ERA was 1.88.

The Yankees did not win their division but made the playoffs. They played against the Cleveland

Here is how Mariano grips a baseball to throw his cutter.

Indians. The Indians beat the Yankees, three games to two.

Mariano gave up a homerun in the bottom of the ninth to finish off New York's hopes to go back to the World Series. This reminded him that he was not perfect, and that he needed to continue to work hard.

As he walked off the mound, he thought "I am going to do all I can to make sure it doesn't happen again." It almost never did.

The Yankees came back driven to win it all again in 1998, and did they ever succeed! Mariano was out on the injured list for two weeks early in the season, but it did not matter to him or to the team. They were both, far and away, the best in baseball that year.

New York won 114 games and lost only 48. Mariano won three games, lost none, and saved 36. He was also great in the post-season, with six saves and 13.1 scoreless innings.

The Yankees beat the Rangers in three straight in the first round of the playoffs, then they got back at the Indians by beating them for the American League title. The Yankees were on their way to another World Series!

Mariano's biography cover featured him preparing to throw his signature cutter.

New York played the San Diego Padres for the title. The way that this year had gone, the Padres had no chance against the Yankees. New York won the Series in four games, which is called a sweep.

This was also the first year that the Yankees' "core four," Rivera, Andy Pettitte, Derek Jeter and Mariano's old catcher from Columbus, Jorge Posada, all played parts in winning the title. There would be many other great moments over the next 15 years.

1999 was another important moment in Mariano's career, as he would get the nickname for which he is remembered. During the 1998 World Series, the Yankees' noticed how the closer for the Padres, Trevor Hoffman would enter the game to the song, "Hell's Bells." The music was loud and powerful, and the hope was to scare opponents because a great pitcher was coming to the mound.

The fans in San Diego would get loud and excited when they heard the song.

The Yankees wanted to try something similar with Mariano. At first, they tried "Welcome to the Jungle," but that one did not quite work. In July of

1999, a worker at the stadium suggested "Enter Sandman" by the band Metallica.

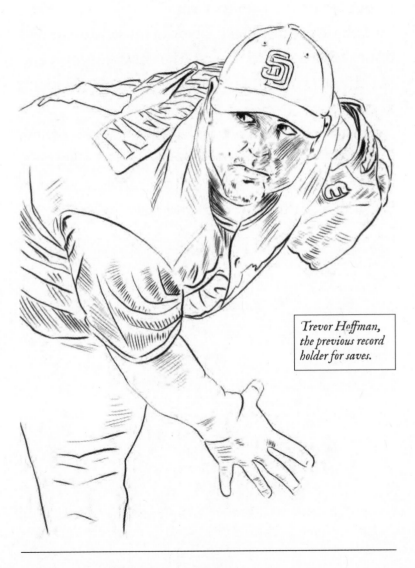

Trevor Hoffman, the previous record holder for saves.

That one did the trick and the fans went wild. The Yankees' fans believed that Mariano was coming in to put the other team to sleep!

This was not Mariano's type of music, and he was not asked about the choice. The song was loud and got the crowd excited. That was the goal. Mariano accepted it.

In that same season, he felt that he had become too proud, and he heard the voice of the Holy Spirit. In one of the first games after the Yankees began to use "Enter Sandman," Mariano blew the save.

Although not his type of music, Mariano accepted the use of the song "Enter Sandman." Here, he stands with the band Metallica.

He responded by saying "I am sorry that I have gotten carried away with my own sense of importance."

He had learned an important lesson. He would be humble and allow himself to be guided by God. He gave up only one more run that entire year.

CHAPTER SEVEN

Important Life Lessons

While Mariano played, the Yankees won the World Series five times: 1996, 1998, 1999, 2000 and 2009. They also lost the Series in 2001 and 2003.

In 1999 Mariano was named the Most Valuable Player for the Series; he saved three of the four wins and had an ERA of 0.00. The people back home in Panama were very proud of him. The people of New York loved him.

So much success could make one feel very self-important. Mariano was different. He remembered to be humble and knew that God guided his steps. He fought hard to win, but never forgot that the hitters he faced, and the persons he dealt with, were people, just like him.

There were some key moments during these years that reminded him to be humble and to forgive others. During these years, these moments affirmed for Mariano the importance of his faith.

In 1998, Mariano and Clara decided to buy a house in New York. They went to a nice part of town and had a friend with them to help. The three of them were dressed in jeans and t-shirts.

When the sales agent opened the door, she was surprised. It was clear that she thought that the Riveras could not afford the house and tried to shoo them out.

Mariano realized that they were being profiled.

The Rivera's house is in White Plains, New York, which is about twenty-five miles from Yankee Stadium.

That is what happens when you judge someone because of how they are dressed or how they look. As soon as the agent found out who the Riveras where, she became very friendly.

It could have been easy for Mariano and Clara to have been upset, but they forgave the agent for her mistake.

"I could have let the flash of anger I felt get the better of me. But I do not. I am far from perfect. So, I forgive, just as the Lord forgives me."

They bought the house.

Another lesson took place because of something

The "core four" who helped lead a great era in Yankees' history. Mariano, Jorge Posada, Andy Pettitte, and Derek Jeter.

that was happening in baseball. Some players, it was discovered, were using drugs called steroids to make themselves stronger and faster. Because of this, they would do better and, hopefully, earn more money.

Mariano was asked about this, and he said that he never used steroids. After all, his beliefs taught him to always be honest and to respect other people.

For those players who got caught, Mariano thought they "should accept your punishment and shut up."

Others asked Mariano what he would do if a teammate used drugs. His answer was very significant.

"I am not going to coddle you...But I am not also going to abandon you."

Mariano knew that all of us are human, and we sometimes make mistakes. The main thing to do is to admit that you have done something wrong and make amends.

Mariano, as a friend and teammate, would stand by you to help you get back on the right path. He would do this with a good friend, pitcher Andy Pettitte, who did use steroids and was sorry he did. Mariano helped him during this difficult time.

Another lesson on being there to help others

came in 1999 when the Yankees were playing the Braves in the Series. A good friend, Paul O'Neill's father died just before Game 4.

Mariano wanted to help Paul, but the team had to play. The Yankees won, and the clubhouse was celebrating. Mariano went over to Paul and told his teammate how sorry he was about his father. Paul was very thankful and said he knew that his dad was watching and was proud of his son and the rest of the Yankees.

This was a fine example of being there to help a friend, but also taking care of the responsibilities

The flags fly at half-staff at Yankee Stadium to honor those who died on 9/11.

that he had at that moment in time.

On September 11, 2001, some terrible events happened in the United States, and the whole

Luis Gonzalez's hit against Mariano won Game Seven of the 2001 World Series for the Arizona Diamondbacks.

country was in shock. The worst of these incidents took place in New York City.

The fact that the Yankees went to another Series just a few weeks later was perceived as a sign of hope by New Yorkers.

Mariano had another great season, with 50 saves and 4 victories. His ERA was 2.34. The Yankees beat the Oakland A's and the Seattle Mariners in the playoffs and then played the Arizona Diamondbacks in the Series. The Series went back and forth, and it all came down to Game 7 in Phoenix.

In this game, the Yankees were leading 2-1 going into the ninth. Mariano had come into the game in the eighth inning and struck out the side. Who better to have on the mound to help win this final game? It did not work out that way.

Mariano gave up a hit to start the inning, then made a fielding error. A couple of batters later, he gave up a double, which tied the game.

Next, he hit a batter and the bases were loaded. Finally, Mariano gave up one last hit to Luis Gonzalez, and Arizona won the game and the Series.

Mariano was sad, but he talked to the press and

The Sandman comes in to close out a game for the Yankees.

took responsibility. He did the best he could, but on that day, it was not enough. As usual, he believed that the Lord guided life and that, even though he did not understand why this had happened, there was a reason for the event.

Shortly after the Series, he understood. If the Yankees had won, a teammate, Enrique Wilson, would have stayed longer in New York. Since there was not a celebration, Enrique and his family left earlier. The flight that they were supposed to be on had an accident and many people died.

One final life lesson during this time came in 2004 while the Yankees were playing the Red Sox for the American League title. Then, two terrible things happened.

First, there was an accident in Mariano's house in Puerto Caimito, and two members of Clara's family were killed. Clara could not pass this information along until after the game. Then, Mariano heard the terrible news. He and Clara flew to Panama for the funerals.

On October 12, 2004, Mariano flew back to New York and helped the Yankees win Game 2 the next night. They would win again on the 16th and led three games to none.

Mariano felt that the best way to honor his relatives was to compete. It seemed that New York was going to yet another World Series.

Then, another awful event happened. The Red Sox came back and won four straight games to win the American League title. This had never happened before!

The Yankees were very upset. Mariano did not get much of a chance to contribute over the last few games. Still, he finished with a 1.29 ERA against Boston.

Mariano learned a great deal from the events described here. He understood, and put into practice, how important it was to be willing to forgive, to be there to help others, and to deal with difficult moments in life.

His faith, and the love of his family, friends and teammates helped him move forward. He was firm in his viewpoints and continued to work hard for his team. The best parts of his career, and a few other bumps, were still to come his way.

CHAPTER EIGHT

Final World Series and Moving up the List of Relievers

When the Red Sox beat the Yankees in 2004, they then won the World Series for the first time since 1918. The fans in Boston were happy, and it was sweet for the Sox to have beaten the Yankees along the way.

At the start of the 2005 season, the Yankees opened in Boston. Before the game, the Boston fans let Mariano have it. They cheered because the Red Sox got back at a team and a player that had beaten them many times before.

Mariano played along. After all, the Red Sox won fair and square, and it was right for them to enjoy their title. This did not mean that Mariano and the Yankees would not try to beat their great rivals in the future.

Mariano did not have a good start to 2005 as he failed in his first two chances for saves. Even the Yankee Stadium fans booed when he lost a lead in one game.

He then converted his next 31 chances. He saved 43 games, won 7, and the Yankees won their division for the 9th straight year. They lost in the playoffs against the Los Angeles Angels.

The Yankees won their division each season until 2008; a total of nine straight years. They did not do well in the playoffs, however, losing in the first round in 2005, 2006, and 2007. New York failed to make the playoffs in 2008.

All through these years, Mariano performed well, as he saved 34, 30, and 39 games.

In 2007, there was a very important moment for Mariano and Clara and it caused a dispute with Joe Torre.

The Yankees were going to play the Rockies in Denver, but at that same time, Mariano Jr. was scheduled to graduate from middle school. Mariano wanted to be there to share the moment.

Joe Torre and Mariano Rivera.

He asked Torre for permission to attend. His manager told Mariano that he would have to go to Colorado instead. After all, his teammates were counting on him to play against Colorado.

Mariano was upset and said he was going to attend the ceremony, with or without permission. This was very important to him because he had not completed his formal schooling. Mariano wanted his sons to know how much he and Clara valued education.

After a while, however, Mariano calmed down and realized "that I cannot defy my manager. . . . It's just not how I operate."

Mariano then spoke with his son and explained that he had to live up to his duties.

"Baseball has given our family an awful lot, but the schedule is not very forgiving."

After the 2007 season Joe Torre left the Yankees and a new manager, Joe Girardi, took over. Girardi, a former catcher, had played with Mariano with the Yankees between 1996 and 1999.

The year 2008 marked the last season that the team played in Yankee Stadium. This was a place where New York played for 85 years and won 26 World Series.

The final game was played on September 21st. The Yankees played against another rival, the Baltimore Orioles. They won 7-3, and Mariano had the honor of being the last man to pitch on the mound of the old ballpark.

The team also gave him the bench from the bullpen as a gift. Mariano sat there for many years and had many fond memories of his times on that piece of wood!

The old home stadium for the Yankees was built in 1923.

As the team opened the new stadium, there would be other changes, as the Yankees brought in some new players. They lost the first game in their new ballpark, but things went well in 2009.

Mariano did his part, saving 44 and winning 3. At one point, he saved 36 straight. His ERA was 1.76.

The team won their division again and finished with 103 wins. They defeated the Twins and the Angels in the playoffs and went to the Series against

The bullpen at old Yankee Stadium. Mariano spent many days here waiting for his turn to close out games.

The new home stadium for the Yankees can hold almost 55,000 people!

the Philadelphia Phillies. In the American League playoffs, Mariano saved three games and had ERAs of 0.00 against Minnesota, and 1.29 against Los Angeles.

This World Series was another magic moment. Mariano saved two games and had a 0.00 ERA as the Yankees defeated the Phillies, four games to two.

Even more important, it was a chance to play on this stage again for the first time since 2003, when the Yankees lost to the Florida Marlins.

Mariano remembered that "I have a new appreciation of how hard it is to get here."

In Game 6, Mariano, as usual, was on the mound

for the ninth frame. The Yankees were ahead, 7 – 3. Mariano mowed down Philadelphia as the final out was an easy ground ball.

As first baseman Mark Teixeira collected the ball, Mariano jumped for joy. This was the fourth time he had gotten the last out in a World Series. Even more importantly, Clara, Mariano Jr., Jafet and their youngest son Jaziel, plus Mariano's and Clara's parents, were there to see the action.

Upon their return home, Mariano got on his knees and thanked God for being so good to him.

Mariano and Mark Teixeira jump for joy after the final out of the 2009 World Series against the Philadelphia Phillies.

In 2010, Mariano and the Yankees prepared to defend their title. Before he started the season, he got to meet Jackie Robinson's widow, Rachel; the man whose number Mariano wore with such pride.

Mariano spends a moment with Rachel Robinson, the widow of Jackie Robinson.

He admitted that there was "pressure...living up to the measure of a man who changed the world and conducted himself with dignity every step of the way."

Once Mariano retired, no one else will ever wear this number in baseball again.

This same year, another special moment came when the Yankees played the Los Angeles Dodgers. The Dodgers, you see, were now managed by Mariano's old friend and manager, Joe Torre.

Mariano and Joe embraced before the game, and Mariano remembered how much Joe had believed in him. He was a man who gave him a chance, and Mariano was very grateful.

Mariano did well in both 2010 and 2011, saving 33 and 44 games. The Yankees made the playoffs both years but fell short of the Series. They lost in the second round to the Texas Rangers in 2010 and then to the Detroit Tigers in the first round in 2011.

Mariano saved three games during the 2010 playoffs and did not record a save in the 2011 post season. It turned out that these would be his final appearances in the playoffs.

By the time that Mariano completed the 2011 season, he had a total of 603 saves.

Trevor Hoffman, the pitcher for the Padres mentioned earlier, was the first to reach the 500 and 600 save mark. He retired in 2010 with 601.

Mariano now had the record for most saves. How many more would he get? How much longer would he play?

CHAPTER NINE

A Bad Injury, a Return, and a Chair of Broken Bats

For the New York Yankees, making the playoffs does not equal success. Over their history, they have won more World Series (27) than any other team.

By 2017, there had been 113 World Series and the Yankees had played in 40. The next closest team in terms of wins and times played were the St. Louis Cardinals; with 11 and 19.

New York made the playoffs in 2011 but hoped for another trip to the Series in 2012. Mariano, of course, expected to be a big part of the effort.

Mariano had not started out as a pitcher, and he liked to play in the outfield to "shag" (catch) fly balls. During batting practice, he often went out and caught flies to get loose.

In early May of 2012, this is what he was doing as the Yankees were set to play the Kansas City Royals. He was goofing around with his teammates and all was normal. Then, something happened.

A fly ball came toward Mariano and, as he had done many times before, he turned and chased the drive. He was at the warning track about to make the catch when he turned to his left and felt a sharp pain through his right knee.

"It's the most pain I have ever felt."

At first, teammates thought Mariano was kidding, but they soon realized that he was in much pain. He was taken from the field on a cart and taken to a hospital.

There, doctors performed a scan of his knee. The injury was serious. Mariano was now 42 years old and wondered if this was the end of his career.

The doctors told him he had torn two ligaments

in his knee. A ligament is a tissue in the body that connects one bone to another. Mariano had torn the bands that joined his knee to his thigh and shin bones.

Although the way to deal with this injury has improved, it still meant Mariano would have surgery, and he would be out for the rest of the 2012 season. He cried as he told his teammates that he would not

Mariano in pain after his knee injury on the warning track in Kansas City.

be able to help them for the rest of the year. Derek Jeter and Andy Pettitte were upset and hugged their old friend.

Mariano turned to the Lord at this difficult moment, as he had always done since he was a teen. The doctor who saw him in the hospital in Kansas City was also a Christian and prayed with him. The doctor's words gave Mariano comfort.

"Lord, please help Mariano heal and give him the strength....to recover from his injury and get back on the mound. Amen." Mariano was very grateful, but he also was prepared to move on.

The reporters who cover the team asked Mariano if he would return for the 2013 season. Mariano said he would.

"'Write it down in big letters. I can't go out this way,' I tell the reporters. 'Miracles happen. I'm a positive man.'"

If there is someone in baseball who knows about miracles, it is Mariano Rivera. His surgery took place on June 12th.

When an athlete is hurt and has surgery, the most painful part of the process is usually not the operation itself; it is the work needed to get back into shape. This process is called rehabilitation, or "rehab" for short.

For Mariano this meant three hours of work on his knee four or five times a week. He stretched, pulled, and pushed to make it strong again.

In the middle of all this pain and stress, there were benefits. Mariano was, for the first time, able to spend a lot of time with Clara, Mariano Jr., Jafet, and Jaziel during the months of the regular season.

While injured, Mariano enjoyed being with his family.

He enjoyed this very much.

He was now certain that the time to finish his career had not yet come, but when it did, he would be fine.

The Yankees, while missing their great closer, still did well in 2012. They once again won their division and made the playoffs.

The Yankees defeated the Baltimore Orioles in the first round but lost to the Detroit Tigers for the American League title.

Once again, they fell short of the World Series. They were proud to have gone far without their closer, but this was not the result they hoped for. Hopefully, Mariano would be back to help them in 2013.

In the spring of 2013, Mariano was back for spring training in Tampa. It felt good to be back, but there was also a new thought in his mind.

He was a homebody and had gotten used to being with Clara and the boys while he recovered. Though his knee and body felt strong, even at age 43, he realized that this was the end of the career line.

On March 9, he announced that this season would, indeed, be his last.

All teams do their best to win, and sometimes rivalries are heated. However, one good thing about baseball is that, when a great player says he is leaving the field for good, many rivals will pay him well-earned praises.

So it was with Mariano. As the Yankees visited the different ballparks that year, the home teams gave Mariano some gifts.

In Cleveland, the home of the Rock 'n' Roll Hall of Fame, the Indians gave him a gold record of "Enter Sandman."

The New York Yankees' spring training home in Tampa.

The Minnesota Twins present Mariano with a rocking chair made of broken bats. This was a tribute to the effectiveness of his cutter.

In Boston, the Red Sox gave him the number 42 from their old scoreboard.

In Minneapolis, the Twins presented him with a rocking chair made from broken bats. This was because the movement of the cutter often jammed hitters and turned their bats into splintered heaps of wood. There were many others.

Mariano, in turn, also decided that he wanted to visit with people who had been important to him at these ballparks. He did not meet with other players or important persons.

Instead, he visited with the men and women who sold tickets, snacks, mowed the field, and kept the locker rooms clean. He wanted them to know how much he valued their help over the years.

On September 22nd, the time to end the career was at hand. The Yankees gave Mariano many gifts

Mariano Rivera day featured many souvenirs, like bobbleheads, hats, and T-shirts.

The Yankees retired Mariano's number on "Mariano Rivera Day," September 22, 2013 at Yankee Stadium.

and almost 50,000 fans roared their approval on "Mariano Rivera Day."

They even retired his number while he was still an active player. That is highly unusual.

Then, on September 26th, the Yankees were in their home park playing the Tampa Bay Rays. Tampa was leading 4-0 in the eighth inning and had two runners on.

Manager Girardi called on the bullpen and Rivera came in for the final time. He shut down the Rays in that inning. He then got out the first two Rays hitters in the ninth.

Then, to his surprise, Derek Jeter and Andy Pettitte came out to get him from the mound. The crowd roared again.

The Yankees still had three more games to play in the season, and Girardi told Mariano it was his choice to pitch again or not. The Yankees did not make the playoffs, so there would not be another chance to pitch in Yankee Stadium.

Before his final turn pitching, Rivera kneeled down in the bullpen and thanked God.

Mariano decided not to take the mound in Houston, wanting his final time on the rubber to be in his home park.

He finished the year with 44 saves, and 6 wins. Those, plus the five saves and one win before his injury in 2012, closed out his career.

Derek Jeter and Andy Pettitte come to the mound to take get Mariano on his final time on the Yankee Stadium mound.

CHAPTER TEN

The Closer Continues to Save

The figures for Mariano Rivera's career are remarkable. In 19 seasons in the Majors, he won 82 games and lost 60.

While the number of wins is not amazing, recall that he was a starter for just a little while. He was a closer for most of his career. Usually, closers do not get wins, just saves.

He pitched in 1115 games and covered 1283.2 innings. He struck out 1173 hitters, and his overall ERA was 2.21. He totaled 652 saves over his career. He is only one of six pitchers to have saved more than 400 games.

He played on five World Series winners (and two other Series where the Yankees lost). He went to the All-Star game 13 times. He was a World Series

Because Mariano was such a great reliever, the Reliever of the Year Award bears his name.

Most Valuable Player (in 1999) and an American League Championship Series Most Valuable Player (in 2003). He was the reliever of the year five times.

In the playoffs, he did his best pitching. In total, he won 8 games, and lost 1, and had 42 saves. His ERA in the playoffs was 0.70.

There is no doubt that when he is eligible (in 2019), he will be a member of the Hall of Fame. It is difficult to think that too many of the voters who select the players for the Hall would vote against Mariano's entry! In fact, he was chosen with 100% of the vote!

Not bad for a poor kid from Puerto Caimito, Panama who started out smelling of fish.

Many times, when a player retires, he is left without a lot to do. After all, he has been an athlete and has played in big games under bright lights. This is not the case for Mariano.

Starting in 1999, he and Clara began efforts to give back to their community and to help those in need. They started the Mariano Rivera Foundation and have been helping poor and underprivileged children and adults with resources, learning centers, and scholarships.

One important effort are book bag drives. These efforts help provide poor children with pencils, paper and other supplies so that they can start the school year ready to learn.

Throughout their lives, Mariano and Clara have been very open about their faith. Clara felt the call to be a minister, and for a time the Riveras ran a small church out of their own home. Soon, there were too many people who wanted to attend to fit in the building. So, they began to look for a larger space.

The outside of the Refuge of Hope Church that Mariano and Clara fixed up in New Rochelle, New York.

This led to another effort; the reconstruction of an old church building in New Rochelle, New York. This is a city near the Bronx, which is where Yankee Stadium stands.

Before he retired, Mariano had heard about this old church building from a friend. The building was over 100 years old and had been empty since the 1970s. It is next to the police station in New Rochelle and had been used to store equipment.

Mariano recalled what it looked like the first time he entered. "Just about everything was in disrepair. There were holes in the roof, and windows . . . more debris and neglect than you can imagine."

While the building was in bad shape, Mariano

felt the presence of the Lord. "In spite of the horrid condition, I saw only beauty. . . . Ankle deep in garbage, surrounded by shards of windows and busted pews, I called Clara." She became the pastor of Refugio de Esperanza which translates to Refuge of Hope.

The new church, with Clara as lead pastor, opened in March of 2014. It is a place where the Riveras share their faith and will to help others with their members. Their goal is to "present the message of salvation to its attendees, but also to provide programs that would meet the needs of the less fortunate in the community."

Mariano visits with students and ballplayers at Roberto Clemente High in Chicago.

In addition to his work in this church, Mariano travels to many places to encourage young people to do their best in all parts of their lives.

An example of this work happened in May of 2017. Mariano went to visit with the Roberto Clemente High School baseball team in the West Town/Humboldt Park area of Chicago.

He talked to these boys about baseball, of course, and some of his experiences on the field. He spoke even more, however, about the value of education and the need for them to be positive role models in their community.

Mariano was inducted into the Baseball Hall of Fame in 2019, drawing a unanimous vote. He was also honored with the Presidential Medal of Freedom, the highest non-military award in the United States.

Mariano also shared with the players how he had insisted that his son, Mariano Jr.complete his degree at Iona University. He had been drafted by the Yankees and then the Washington Nationals.

Mariano's talk had an impact on a pitcher name Pedro Cora. "He showed me more of an experience of how he grew up, with Jesus and how him playing baseball was good for him growing up." Hopefully, Mariano planted a seed of hope with Pedro that will help him as he grows up.

Other events that Mariano has participated in include helping to get more kids to play baseball in Panama. He also hosted a charity ball to raise money to benefit the Panama City Children's Hospital.

While he has earned a chance to relax, Mariano (and Clara) continue to give to their community, our nation, and to the people of Panama.

Mariano Rivera Jr. pitching for the Iona University Gaels. He is now pitching in the farm system of the Washington Nationals.

The story of Mariano Rivera on the mound of professional baseball may not be over yet, however. Mariano Jr. pitched for the Iona University Gaels and in 2015 was named the pitcher of the year in the Metro Atlantic Conference. He set a team record that year with 113 strike outs.

Does he use his dad's pitch (the cutter)? No, he relies on his fastball, changeup and slider.

"I've been working on that, and my father has helped. But I'll never be able to throw it like him. That's his pitch."

In 2016, Mariano Jr. pitched in the South Atlantic League All-Star Game. As of 2018, Mariano Jr. was pitching for the Potomac Nationals of the A-level Carolina League.

No doubt, being the son of a legend must be very difficult, especially if you play the same position as your dad did. Because of this, Mariano Jr. works very hard to be as good of a pitcher as possible. He is also very religious, just like his parents.

"I want to be able to pray every day. I want to be able to read my Bible every day. That's a big part of my life."

In both areas, Mariano Jr. has big shoes to fill. He has had a great example, both on and off the field, from his parents.

The Sandman coming in to close out a game for the Yankees became immortalized in a keepsake pin in 2013.

Mariano Rivera will long be remembered as one of the greatest pitchers in the history of baseball. He was poor, did not think he had a future in baseball, but because of his determination and faith, he was able to do many great things. He is a proud Panamanian, who is always ready to help his fellow man.

He broke a lot of bats along the way and helped create one of the greatest eras in New York Yankee history. There is much that can be learned from his life story. Believe in yourself, respect others, work hard, and put forth your best effort in everything you do.

Who knows how far you will go? Mariano faced many challenges and look how much he has done in his life!

I don't just think regular season. I think playoffs. World Series. That's how I think.

I think the good Lord is a Yankee.

I'm not used to seeing the ball go wherever she wants. As a pitcher, I like to be—I don't want to say perfect, but I want to know what the ball is going to do.

I learned early in my life that sometimes I'm going to lose. I don't like it, but I accept it, meaning that I understand it's going to happen. But I don't see it like defeat; I see it like a learning process. Then if there's nothing to learn, I move on.

I get over bad games right away. Sometimes I've let it go even before I've left the mound. That quick. Why? Because it's over. What can you do about it? Nothing. The only thing you can do is fight if you're still in the game. After that you can do nothing.

All around me are guys who have been groomed to do this for a decade or more, and here I am, a guy who got here because one Sunday afternoon the Panama Oeste Cowboys needed somebody to finish a game

Bullpen – The area used by pitchers to get loose before they enter a game.

Closer – A relief pitcher who comes in to "close" the game by getting the final few outs.

Colombia – Country that borders on the southeast border of Panama. Before 1903 what is now Panama use to be part of this nation.

Curveball – A pitch that curves from a straight path. This is designed to fool hitters.

Cutter – A version of a fastball that moves slightly away from the pitcher's arm-side. If effective, it can break many bats.

ERA – The average number of runs a pitcher gives up. The lower the number, the better.

Farm system – A series of teams tied to a Major League club who are responsible for providing experience to young ballplayers. Each Major League club has teams in Rookie League, Class A, Class AA, and Class AAA.

Fastball – Most common type of pitch. It is thrown more for speed than for movement.

Iguanas – A large lizard with a spiny crest.

Isthmus – A narrow strip of land with sea on either side linking two larger areas of land.

Ligament – A band of tissue that connects two bones or holds together a joint like the knee.

Machete – A long heavy knife used to cut sugar cane and other things. Can be used as a weapon.

Mound – Raised section of the ballfield where the pitcher stands.

No-hitter – A game in which the pitcher of one team does not give up any hits. This is not a common event.

Outhouse – A building outside of a house containing a toilet. Typically, there is no plumbing.

Panama Canal – Canal that crosses the narrowest portion of the Isthmus of Panama. Connects the Atlantic and Pacific Oceans.

Profiled – Assuming that a person has certain traits given how they look or dress.

Rehabilitation (or Rehab) – The process of helping a person who has had an injury restore lost skills and abilities.

Rivals – Two teams that are trying to achieve the same goal, and that like to beat each other. The Yankees and Red Sox are the most important rivalry in baseball.

Room Service – A service provided by hotels to guests which bring food and drink to their rooms.

Rubber – A white rubber strip from which the pitcher pushes off in order to gain speed toward home plate.

Scout – A person whose job it is to look for talent for the various Major League teams.

"Set up" Reliever – The reliever who pitches, usually, one or two innings before the closer enters the game.

Shagging baseballs – Catching flyballs in the outfield before a game in order to get loose.

Sliders – A fast pitch that usually curves in the direction opposite to the pitcher's arm

Steroids – A type of chemical that many ballplayers used to become stronger and run faster. Use of steroids is not permitted by the Major Leagues.

Water pumps – A pump used to circulate water. In a boat like the Lisa, the pumps keep water out of the boat so that it will stay afloat.

1969

1969 November 29: Mariano Rivera is born.

1990-1999

1990 February 17: The New York Yankees sign Mariano Rivera.

1991 November 9: Mariano and Clara marry.

1992 August 27: Mariano has surgery on his right elbow.

1993 October 4: After Clara suffered from chicken pox, Mariano Rivera Jr. is born healthy.

1995 May 23: Mariano makes his Major League debut against the California Angels in Anaheim, California.

1995 June 11: Mariano and Derek Jeter are sent back down to the Columbus Clippers by the New York Yankees.

1995 July 4: Mariano makes his first start since being recalled to the Majors against the Chicago White Sox. He gives up two hits in 8 innings, and strikes out 11.

1996 May 17: Mariano records the first save of his career against the California Angels.

1996: Carla gives birth to Jafet.

1997 September 30: Mariano earns the first of his record 42 post-season saves against the Cleveland Indians.

1999 October 27: Mariano is named Most Valuable Player for the 1999 World Series.

2003: Jaziel, the Rivera's youngest son is born.

2004 May 28: Mariano records his 300th save against the Tampa Bay Rays.

2004 October 10-12: Mariano and Clara attend the funerals of her cousins, Victor Dario Avila and his son, Victor Leonel, who were electrocuted at the Rivera's Puerto Caimito house. Later that night, he pitches against the Red Sox in the American League Championship Series.

2006 July 16: Mariano records his 400th save against the Chicago White Sox.

2008 October 7: Mariano has surgery on his right shoulder.

2009 June 28: Mariano records his 500th save against the New York Mets.

2009 November 4: Mariano records the final out of the World Series versus the Philadelphia Phillies. This was the fourth time he threw the last pitch in a Yankee World Series victory.

2011 September 14: Mariano records his 600th save.

2011 September 17: Mariano records his 601st save against the Toronto Blue Jays, tying San Diego Padres' reliever, Trevor Hoffman.

2011 September 19: Mariano records his record-breaking 602nd save against the Minnesota Twins.

2012 May 3-4: Mariano suffers torn ligaments in his right knee at Kaufmann Stadium in Kansas City, Missouri. The next day, he announces that he will return from this injury.

2013 March 9: Mariano announces that 2013 will be his final season in the Majors.

2013 July 16: Mariano makes his 13th, and final, appearance in the All-Star Game.

2013 September 22: The team hold "Mariano Rivera Day" at Yankee Stadium.

2013 September 26: Mariano pitches in his final game at Yankee Stadium.

2015 June 9: Mariano Jr. is drafted by the Washington Nationals.

1968 October: General Omar Torrijos leads a coup and takes over the government of Panama.

1969 July 20-24: The lunar module Eagle lands on the lunar surface. Neil Armstrong takes the first walk on the moon. Astronauts return safely to Earth.

1972 December 31: Roberto Clemente dies in a plane crash off of the coast of Puerto Rico.

1973 January 1: George Steinbrenner buys the New York Yankees from CBS.

1973 April 4: The World Trade Center opens in New York City.

1977 July 13: New York City blackout darkens the city for 25 hours.

1979 November 4: Iran Hostage Crisis begins. It will last 444 days.

1980 February 22: The US Olympic hockey team defeats the Soviet Union team. This is known as the "Miracle on Ice."

1981 October 28: The band Metallica forms in Los Angeles.

1983 August 12: General Manuel Noriega becomes the leader of Panama behind a civilian government.

1983 October 25: Microsoft Word is first released to the public.

1987 August 9: The first night game takes place at Wrigley Field in Chicago.

1989 April 1: Bill White becomes president of the National League. The first African American to head a major American sports league.

1989 December 20: United States invades Panama.

1992 April 9: A Miami jury convicts former Panamanian leader, Manuel Noriega, of assisting Colombia's drug cartel.

1993 February 26: Bombing of World Trade Center in New York City.

1995 March 1: Yahoo! is founded in Santa Clara, California.

1999 February 12: President Bill Clinton is impeached. He is acquitted by the Senate.

2000 December 12: After a contested election, the Supreme Court ends the recount of votes in Florida, thus making George W. Bush the winner of the 2000 presidential election.

2001 September 11: The attacks on the Twin Towers in New York City leaves about 3000 people dead.

2001 November 4: Mariano blows the save in the 7th game of the World Series against the Diamondbacks. He gives up a game-winning single to Luis Gonzalez in the bottom of the 9th.

2001 November 12: Flight 587, the flight Enrique Wilson and his family were supposed to take, crashes in Queens, N.Y. 260 people died.

2005 February 15: YouTube goes online.

2006 March 6-20: The first World Baseball Classic is held.

2007 December 13: The Mitchell Report, which accuses 89 current or retired Major Leaguers of using steroids, is released.

2009 January 20: Barrack Obama is sworn in as President.

2011 September 11: The National September 11 Memorial and Museum opens in New York City ten years after the attack.

2014 November 3: The new One World Trade Center building opens in New York City.

2016 July 3: Major League Baseball plays a game on a military base, Ft. Bragg, N.C., for the first time ever.

2016 November 8: Donald Trump is elected President.

2017 September 20: Hurricane Maria makes landfall in Puerto Rico

Baseball-Reference.com.

Blum, Ronald. "Mariano Rivera's Legacy: How a Slim Shortstop from Panama Became a Cooperstown Caliber Closer for the New York Yankees, September 28, 2013. See: http://nationalpost.com/sports/baseball/mlb/ mariano-riveras-legacy-how-a-slim-shortstop-from- panama-became-a-cooperstown-calibre-closer-for-the- new-york-yankees.

DePaolo, Joe. "A Son of the Game: Mariano Rivera III Tries to Make a Name for Himself," May 28, 2014. See: https://www.sbnation.com/ longform/2014/5/28/5744888/mariano-rivera-iii-profile.

Fangraphs.com.

Fitzgerald, Jim. "Mariano Rivera Rescues, Renovates a New Rochelle Church," March 7, 2014. See: https:// www.lohud.com/story/news/local/westchester/new- rochelle/2014/03/06/mariano-rivera-rescues-renovates- new-rochelle-church/6112961/.

Mariano Rivera Foundation website. See: https:// themarianoriverafoundation.org/.

Masterson, Matt. "Former Yankee Great Mariano Rivera Talks Baseball, Life with CPS Students," May 16, 2017. See: https://chicagotonight.wttw.com/2017/05/16/ former-yankee-great-mariano-rivera-talks-baseball-life-cps- students.

Miller, Lisa, "Saved," June 9, 2013. See: http://nymag. com/news/features/sports/mariano-rivera-2013-6/.

Refugio de Esperanza/Refuge of Hope website. See: http://www.refugiodeesperanza.net/home.

Retrosheet.org.

Rivera, Mariano with Wayne Coffey. *The Closer: My Story*. New York: Back Bay Books, 2014.

Waldstein, David. "Closing Scene: Hugs and Tears in Rivera's Last Home Game," September 26, 2013. See: https://www.nytimes.com/2013/09/27/sports/baseball/closing-scene-hugs-and-tears-in-riveras-last-home-game.html.

Further Reading

McDermott, Terry. *Off Speed: Baseball, Pitching and the Art of Deception*. New York: Pantheon Books, 2017.

Pepe, Phil. *Core Four: The Heart and Soul of the Yankee Dynasty*. Chicago: Triumph Books, 2014.

Jorge Iber is a professor of History at Texas Tech University. His research focuses on the role and importance of Latinos and Latinas in American sport. He has written about athletes who have played at both the professional and amateur levels in sports such as football and baseball.

Raquel Iber has been a teacher in both public and private schools over the last two decades. She is particularly interested in helping students to develop a love of reading so that they may be able to find role models who can help them learn about the world and inspire them to set and achieve goals.